03-0818
$22.95

TOTAL
HOCKEY

BY TODD KORTEMEIER

SportsZone

An Imprint of Abdo Publishing
www.abdopublishing.com

abdopublishing.com

Published by Abdo Publishing, a division of ABDO, PO Box 398166, Minneapolis, Minnesota 55439. Copyright © 2017 by Abdo Consulting Group, Inc. International copyrights reserved in all countries. No part of this book may be reproduced in any form without written permission from the publisher. SportsZone™ is a trademark and logo of Abdo Publishing.

Printed in the United States of America, North Mankato, Minnesota
092016
012017

Cover Photos: Del Marcum/Cal Sport Media/AP Images, foreground; Alex Tois/Shutterstock Images, background
Interior Photos: Alex Tois/Shutterstock Images, 1; Anthony Nesmith/Cal Sport Media/AP Images, 4–5; John Crouch/Icon Sportswire/AP Images, 6, 24; Mike Carlson/AP Images, 9; Alexander Henderson/Library and Archives Canada/C-081683, 10–11; Notman & Son/Library and Archives Canada, 12; AP Images, 14, 30–31, 38–39, 42–43; Paolo Bona/Shutterstock Images, 16–17; Charles Krupa/AP Images, 18; Matthew Jacques/Shutterstock Images, 20–21; Shutterstock Images, 22, 26–27; Peter Bregg/The Canadian Press/AP Images, 28; Gene J. Puskar/AP Images, 32; Library and Archives Canada/PA-074583, 34–35; IHA/Icon SMI/Newscom, 37; Ryn Remiorz/Canadian Press/AP Images, 40; Kevin Sousa/Icon Sportswire/AP Images, 45; Nick Wagner/Cal Sport Media/Newscom, 46–47; Steve Kingsman/Icon Sportswire/AP Images, 49; John Cordes/Icon Sportswire/AP Images, 50; Damon Tarver/Cal Sports Media/AP Images, 52–53; AE/AP Images, 54; Steven Senne/AP Images, 56; Andy Blenkush/Cal Sport Media/Newscom, 58–59; David Hahn/Icon Sportswire/AP Images, 60

Editor: Patrick Donnelly
Series Designer: Jake Nordby

Publisher's Cataloging-in-Publication Data

Names: Kortemeier, Todd, author.
Title: Total hockey / by Todd Kortemeier.
Description: Minneapolis, MN : Abdo Publishing, 2017. | Series: Total sports | Includes bibliographical references and index.
Identifiers: LCCN 2016945689 | ISBN 9781680785050 (lib. bdg.) | ISBN 9781680798333 (ebook)
Subjects: LCSH: Hockey--Juvenile literature.
Classification: DDC 796.962--dc23
LC record available at http://lccn.loc.gov/2016945689

CONTENTS

THE GOAL

Lighting the lamp. Putting the biscuit in the basket. Whatever you call it, scoring a goal is what hockey is all about. Some of the most famous players were great goal scorers. They brought fans to their feet time and again.

The top goal scorers have a few things in common. They know where to be on the ice to get a good shot. They also anticipate puck movement. That means they know where the puck is and where it's probably going next.

The Boston Bruins celebrate "lighting the lamp" after scoring a goal.

There are a few different types of shots. A slap shot is a big, powerful shot. It can travel more than 100 miles per hour (161 km/h). A player winds up for a slap shot, bringing the stick blade well overhead. But it's more difficult to direct a slap shot to a specific spot. A wrist shot or "wrister" is much more accurate. The player puts the stick blade on the puck and quickly thrusts it forward. It's easier to pick out a target with a wrister.

Nobody scored more goals in National Hockey League (NHL) history than Wayne Gretzky. He earned the nickname "The Great One." Gretzky played in the NHL from 1979 through 1999. His career numbers were astounding. He set NHL records with 894 career goals and 92 goals in a single season (1981–82). Gretzky made such

DO OR DIE

Through 2016 only two Stanley Cup Finals series have come down to overtime in Game 7. Pete Babando's goal lifted the Detroit Red Wings past the New York Rangers in 1950. Tony Leswick did the same for Detroit against the Montreal Canadiens four years later.

Brent Burns of the San Jose Sharks prepares to fire a wrist shot.

an impact on the game that his No. 99 was retired throughout the NHL.

Today's NHL features some amazing goal scorers, too. Alex Ovechkin broke into the league with a 52-goal season for the Washington Capitals in 2005–06. He hasn't slowed down since. Ovechkin has led the NHL in goals six times. He scored his 500th career goal in January 2016. Tampa Bay Lightning forward Steven Stamkos scored his 300th career goal one month later. At age 26, Stamkos was the ninth-youngest player to reach 300 in NHL history.

The term "lighting the lamp" refers to the red light behind the net that signals a goal.

The leading goal scorer in the NHL wins the Richard Trophy. It is named for Montreal Canadiens great Maurice "Rocket" Richard. In 1944–45, he was the first NHL player to score 50 goals in a season.

Some of the biggest goals in NHL history are overtime

Steven Stamkos, *right*, celebrates one of his many goals for the Tampa Bay Lightning.

playoff goals. NHL playoff games go to sudden-death overtime if the score is tied after three periods. That means the next goal wins. Teams have clinched the Stanley Cup with an overtime goal 17 times through 2016.

2

BORN IN CANADA

Hockey is a pretty simple game on the surface. Two teams try to get an object into their opponent's goal using a stick. This could describe many games played throughout history. And hockey descended from many of them.

Similar ice games were played in Europe as far back as the 1600s. When Europeans came to North America, they took note of Native American games. One was an early version of lacrosse. These games eventually led to what we now call field hockey. And that game made its way to the ice.

A hockey game on the campus of McGill University during the 1884 Winter Carnival Hockey Tournament in Montreal

A hockey game in Montreal in 1904

In 1872 a Nova Scotia native named James Creighton brought the game to Montreal, Quebec. His friends loved the sport. They played at the Victoria Skating Rink. They played the first indoor hockey game there on March 3, 1875.

The game didn't look much like the hockey we know today. Forward passes were not allowed. The goalie had to stay on his feet. But hockey grew in popularity. The first rules—called the Montreal Rules—were recorded in 1877.

Hockey teams began to pop up throughout Canada and the northern United States. Colleges and athletic clubs sponsored teams in leagues and tournaments. But players didn't get paid in the early days. That changed in 1904. The International Hockey League was founded. It was the world's first professional hockey league. It featured teams from the United States and Canada.

THE OLDEST HOCKEY RINK

Indoor ice rinks are common today. But hockey was played on frozen ponds, lakes, or rivers in its early days. Canada's oldest surviving indoor rink is the Stannus Street Rink in Windsor, Ontario. It was built in 1897.

Soon more leagues began to form. One of the best was the National Hockey Association. That league included the Montreal Canadiens. But by 1917 some team owners were not

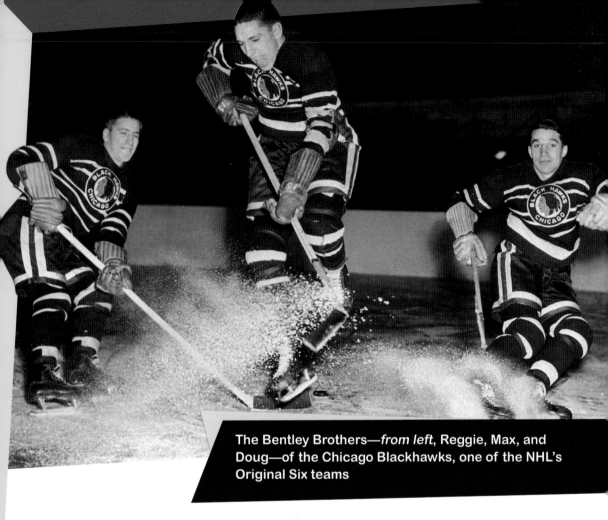

The Bentley Brothers—*from left*, Reggie, Max, and Doug—of the Chicago Blackhawks, one of the NHL's Original Six teams

happy in that league. They decided to form their own league. They gave it a similar name: the National Hockey League.

The NHL started off small. It had four teams in its first season. It eventually grew to six teams. Those six are still in the league today. The Canadiens, Toronto Maple Leafs, Boston Bruins, New York Rangers, Detroit Red Wings, and Chicago Blackhawks are known as the "Original Six."

In 1967 the NHL doubled in size. It added six new teams that year, and it has kept growing. As of 2016, the NHL had 30 teams. That year the league owners voted to expand the league. The newest team would be located in Las Vegas. Seven teams are located in Canada. The rest are in the United States.

The "Original Six" were the only teams in the NHL from 1942–43 until 1966–67.

3 ALL ABOUT EQUIPMENT

Hockey equipment is part safety, part performance. Players have been wearing protective gear since the early days of the sport. Equipment has become both lighter and stronger over time. Players are safer than ever thanks to their high-tech gear.

The first safety gear was simple. Players started wearing shin guards in the 1880s. They added kneepads, elbow pads, shoulder pads, and gloves during the next few decades. Players wear the same equipment today. But now they're made of super-light plastics and fabrics.

The skates are lighter, the sticks are stronger—everything about hockey equipment has improved since the game's earliest days.

Craig MacTavish, shown here in 1990, was the last NHL player to play without a helmet.

Ice skates are older than the game of hockey. Indigenous people made skates using animal bones as blades. These skates didn't carve the ice. But they allowed the user to glide on a frozen surface. Metal skate blades were invented in the 1500s. The blades attached to the bottom of a regular shoe.

It wasn't until 1933 that the Bauer Company started making skates with an attached boot.

Early hockey sticks were carved from a single piece of wood. Almost all sticks were made of wood through the 1950s. Fiberglass sticks started to appear in the 1960s. They were lighter and more durable. Players began using sticks with aluminum shafts in the 1980s. They were heavier, but they hardly ever broke. Today most sticks are made of a light, strong alloy. Wooden sticks have become increasingly rare.

BILL MASTERTON

Professional players once were not required to wear helmets. Bill Masterton of the Minnesota North Stars was one who did not. In a 1968 game against the Oakland Seals, Masterton hit his head on the ice. He died hours later. Masterton is the only NHL player to die from an injury during a game. His death prompted talks about safety. But it took until 1979 for the NHL to require all new players to wear helmets. Players now wear them at every level of hockey.

A skating rink can be any size or shape. But a hockey rink has to have just the right dimensions. And sizes vary depending on the league and level of hockey.

A standard NHL rink is 200 feet (61 m) long and 85 feet (26 m) wide. An Olympic-sized rink is the same length, but it's 100 feet (30.5 m) wide. Olympic-sized ice is used in the Winter Olympic Games as well as other international tournaments.

The corners of a hockey rink are rounded to help keep the puck moving. Faceoffs take place at

Every period starts with a faceoff at center ice.

The New York Rangers began playing in the latest version of Madison Square Garden in 1968.

nine dots spread throughout the ice. There are four dots along each side of the rink. The ninth dot is in the middle of the rink. That's where every hockey game starts.

The oldest arena in the NHL is New York's Madison Square Garden. The home of the New York Rangers opened in 1968.

Most of the other rinks are less than 25 years old. The New York Islanders played their last season at Nassau County Coliseum in 2014–15. The team moved approximately 20 miles (32 km) west to play its home games at Brooklyn's Barclays Center.

Many of the NHL's most historic arenas are now gone. Toronto's Maple Leaf Gardens was the home of the Maple Leafs from 1931 through 1999. Fans filled its steep bleachers to watch the 11-time Stanley Cup winners. The Maple Leafs moved into Air Canada Center in 1999.

OUTDOOR HOCKEY

All hockey used to be played outdoors. Outdoor hockey is a novelty these days. The NHL went back to its roots when it began holding the Winter Classic in 2008. The outdoor game takes place on New Year's Day. It is usually held in a baseball or football stadium. A specially refrigerated rink is laid down on top of the grass or turf. These outdoor games have become very popular with fans and teams.

The Forum in Montreal was another of hockey's most famous arenas. The Canadiens won 24 Stanley Cups in the arena's 70-year history. Its rafters were filled with

championship banners and the retired numbers of Canadiens legends. In 1996 the Canadiens moved into a new arena.

One of the newer rinks in the NHL is Rogers Place in Edmonton, Alberta. The home of the Oilers opened in the fall of 2016. It features a giant high-definition scoreboard.

The NHL launched the Stadium Series in 2014. It allows the league to have more than one outdoor game per year.

The Winter Classic and Stadium Series have brought outdoor hockey back to NHL fans.

5

THE WORLD OF HOCKEY

Hockey is popular around the world. Most NHL players have come from Canada and the United States. However, 39 other countries have sent players to the world's best league. Other countries have high-quality leagues, too.

More than 1.2 million Canadians over the age of 15 play hockey. Canada has some of the best youth hockey programs in the world. Its national team is a major point of pride. The sport is also growing rapidly among female players. From 1990 through 2013, participation in girls' and women's hockey grew by more than 900 percent in Canada.

Children play hockey in Serbia in 2011.

Canada's Paul Henderson shoots against Soviet goalie Vladislav Tretiak, *20*, during the famed 1972 Summit Series.

Hockey has gained a tremendous following in northern Europe and Russia. Russia has an especially long history of top-level hockey. As the Soviet Union, its teams dominated worldwide competitions. Today the Kontinental Hockey League (KHL) features many talented players. Many players have made the jump from the KHL to the NHL. Some have returned to play in the KHL. Ilya Kovalchuk is one such player. He used to play for the New Jersey Devils.

The hockey world was dominated by Canada and the Soviet Union in the 1970s. In 1972 the countries faced each other in the Summit Series. Canada's roster was loaded with future Hall of Famers such as Phil Esposito, Bobby Orr, and Stan Mikita. The Soviet team had won four of the previous five Olympic gold medals.

SWEDISH SURGE

Through the 2015–16 season, Sweden had produced the most NHL players of any country besides Canada and the United States.

The teams played eight games; four in each country. The Soviets got off to a 3–1–1 start before Canada won the last three games in Moscow. The Summit Series showed that hockey's popularity had expanded well beyond North America. But Canada was still a major player.

6

GOING FOR GOLD

Hockey has been an Olympic sport since 1920. Only amateur players were allowed to play most of those years. Professional players were not allowed. Canada won six of the first seven gold medals. But then the Soviet Union began to dominate international hockey.

The Soviet players were professionals in disguise. Many of them were military officers. But their main job was to play hockey. The true amateur players from other countries were outclassed. The Soviets won gold at seven of nine Olympics from 1956 to 1988.

Soviet captain Boris Mayorov, *top center*, and his teammates won the gold medal at the 1968 Winter Olympic Games in Grenoble, France.

The United States won the gold medal in 1960 and 1980. The 1980 victory was one of the biggest upsets in sports history. Team USA was made up of college players. The Americans and Soviets played an exhibition game five days before the Olympics started. The Soviets won 10–3. But in the semifinals the Americans turned the tables. They won 4–3. They won gold two days later by beating Finland.

THE MOST MEDALS

Canada's Jayna Hefford and Hayley Wickenheiser played in the first five women's Olympic hockey tournaments. Each player has five medals. This is the most for any hockey player in Olympic history. Many others have four. Caroline Ouellette is the only other player to have won four gold medals.

In 1998 NHL players and other pros were allowed to play. That put the best players in the world on the ice. Canada has won the most gold medals in men's hockey. In 2014 it won its ninth gold medal in Sochi, Russia. Women's hockey has been in the Olympics since 1998. The United States won the first gold medal. Canada won the next four.

Hayley Wickenheiser celebrates after helping Canada win the women's hockey gold medal at the 2010 Winter Games in Vancouver, Canada.

7

WOMEN IN HOCKEY

Women's hockey is one of the fastest-growing sports in the world. Millions play the sport. More try it every year. Most of this growth has come since 1990. But women have been playing hockey almost since the sport's invention.

Isobel Preston was the first woman photographed playing hockey in 1890. Her father was Lord Stanley of Preston, namesake of the Stanley Cup. The first women's hockey game was played the next year in Ottawa, Canada. College teams started to form in the 1920s. But organized women's hockey didn't take off until the 1980s.

A women's hockey team from Gore Bay, Manitoulin Island, Ontario, in 1921

MANON RHÉAUME

In 1992 Tampa Bay Lightning general manager Phil Esposito went on a scouting trip to Montreal. There he saw a goalie who really impressed him. The goalie was small. But Esposito saw potential. He got a surprise when that goalie turned out to be a woman. Her name was Manon Rhéaume. Esposito invited her to training camp with the Lightning. She performed so well that on September 30, 1992, she became the first woman to play in a preseason NHL game. Rhéaume enjoyed a long minor league career playing against both men and women.

The first women's college tournament took place in 1984. The first international tournament was in 1987. Women got their own World Championship tournament in 1990. But they still were absent from the Olympics. That was corrected in 1998. Six nations competed in the first women's hockey tournament at the Olympics in Nagano, Japan.

College hockey in the United States produces some of the best women's players. Many have played for their national teams at the Olympics. The sport is strong at the amateur level. But few pro leagues exist.

In 2015 the National Women's Hockey League was founded.

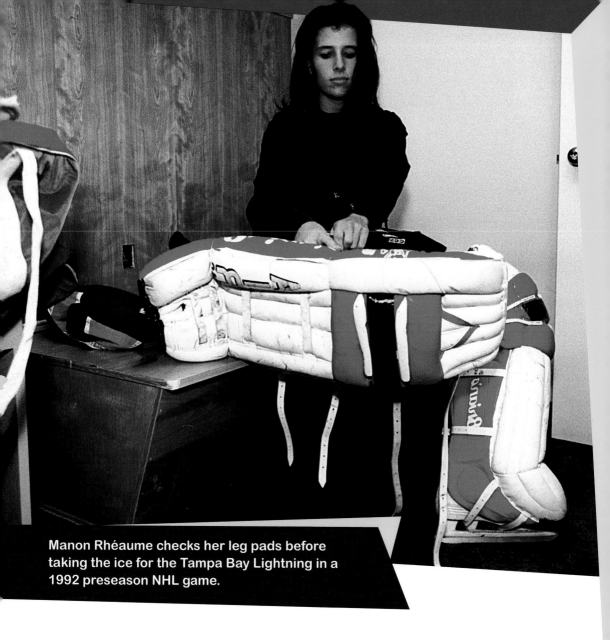

Manon Rhéaume checks her leg pads before taking the ice for the Tampa Bay Lightning in a 1992 preseason NHL game.

The league began with four teams, giving women an opportunity to play professional hockey. It doesn't yet match the opportunities available to men. But it's a step in the right direction for women's pro hockey.

8

THE NETMINDER

Playing goalie is dangerous. Goalies didn't wear masks when the sport first started. They also wore very little padding. It sounds crazy to play without maximum protection against today's 100-mile-per-hour (161 km/h) slap shots. But shots weren't always that fast. And players weren't able to lift the puck as easily.

Goalies didn't start using masks until the 1950s. In 1974 Andy Brown of the Pittsburgh Penguins was the last NHL goalie to play without a mask. Goalie pads have changed. They're lighter and stronger. The leg pads are much bigger, too.

Goalies didn't wear masks in the days of Frank Brimsek, shown here making a save for the Boston Bruins in 1939.

Goaltending styles have also changed. Most goalies in the early days played a "stand-up" style. Stand-up goalies never left their feet. They skated around the crease to turn pucks away.

Montreal Canadiens star Patrick Roy popularized the "butterfly" style in the mid-1980s. Butterfly goalies drop to their knees to stop shots. When they extend their leg pads to the side, they resemble the shape of a butterfly.

Not all goalies play only one style. Dominik Hasek played his own unique style. Hasek relied on his instincts and reflexes. He was constantly in motion around the net.

GOALIES WHO SCORE

A goal by the netminder is a rare event in hockey. It's only happened 14 times in NHL history. Martin Brodeur of the New Jersey Devils scored three times in his career. But only one of his goals came by him shooting the puck into the net. The other two were knocked into the net by the other team. In those cases, Brodeur was simply the last Devil to have touched the puck.

Patrick Roy demonstrates the butterfly goaltending style that he popularized during his career.

9

THE BLUELINERS

All hockey players have some defensive responsibilities. A top goal scorer might find himself stripped of the puck in an instant. Then he must play defense to get the puck back. But the defensemen are the key to a team's defensive effort. Defensemen are usually protecting the blue line when their team has the puck in the offensive zone. When the opponents take possession, defensemen retreat to help protect their zone.

Defensemen have to be great skaters. They must be able to change direction quickly. They need great vision. They also have to know where

Bobby Orr showed hockey fans that defensemen could score, too.

THE TALLEST PLAYER IN NHL HISTORY

It helps for a defenseman to be tall. It means they have a longer reach to poke the puck away. But they don't come much taller than Zdeno Chara. At 6 feet, 9 inches (206 cm), Chara is the tallest player in NHL history. He uses a stick 65 inches (165 cm) long. That's the longest the NHL will allow. But Chara isn't just tall. He is a Norris Trophy winner and one of the league's best defensemen.

the puck is going. One thing they don't necessarily need is size. Most defensemen are pretty big. But smaller players can make up for that with good decisions and great skating.

Some defensemen are pretty good scorers, too. Longtime Boston Bruins great Bobby Orr led the NHL in scoring twice. He also won the Norris Trophy, which is given to the league's best defenseman, every year from 1968 to 1975.

Orr changed the way defense was played. Today if you play like Orr, you're called a "two-way" defenseman. Some of the best two-way defensemen in the game

Zdeno Chara, *33*, stands head and shoulders above his teammates and everybody else in the NHL.

today are P. K. Subban and Erik Karlsson. Both are solid defenders who can also score goals.

10

IN THE BOX

Most sports feature some type of punishment for a team that commits a foul. In basketball, opponents shoot free throws. In football, teams lose yardage. Hockey is unique. The player who committed the foul has to leave the game, at least for a while.

Most hockey penalties are two-minute violations. These are called minor penalties. This could be for tripping or holding an opponent. Delay of game, hooking, high-sticking, and slashing are other common minor penalties. The offending player has to sit in the penalty box, and his team

Tripping is a two-minute minor penalty in hockey.

plays with one fewer player for two minutes. The penalty is over if the other team scores. The player can leave the penalty box and his team returns to full strength.

A major penalty is called for a more serious foul. Some of these are more severe versions of minor penalties. For instance, if you hit an opponent near their neck or head with your stick, that's usually a minor penalty. But if your hit causes your opponent to bleed, it's a major penalty. A player who commits a major foul gets a five-minute penalty. They have to stay in the penalty box while their team plays shorthanded for the full five minutes, no matter how many goals they give up.

Fighting can get players kicked out of a game in other sports. In hockey, it's a major

GORDIE HOWE HAT TRICK

Gordie Howe retired in 1980 as the NHL's all-time leading goal scorer. He was tough. His mix of scoring and physical abilities inspired the so-called "Gordie Howe Hat Trick." It consists of a goal, an assist, and a fight in the same game. Because of incomplete records, no one knows how many times Howe actually did it.

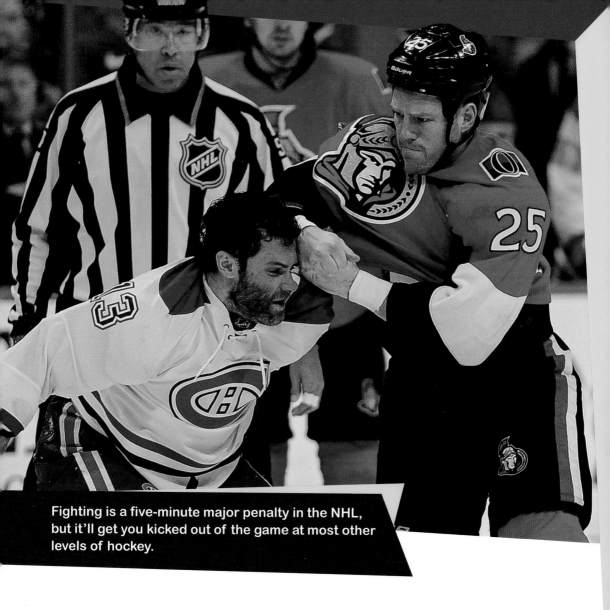

Fighting is a five-minute major penalty in the NHL, but it'll get you kicked out of the game at most other levels of hockey.

penalty at the NHL level. Some professional teams have players whose specialty is fighting. These players are called "enforcers." They try to protect their teammates by fighting. In theory, other teams won't rough up star players if they know they'll have to deal with the enforcer.

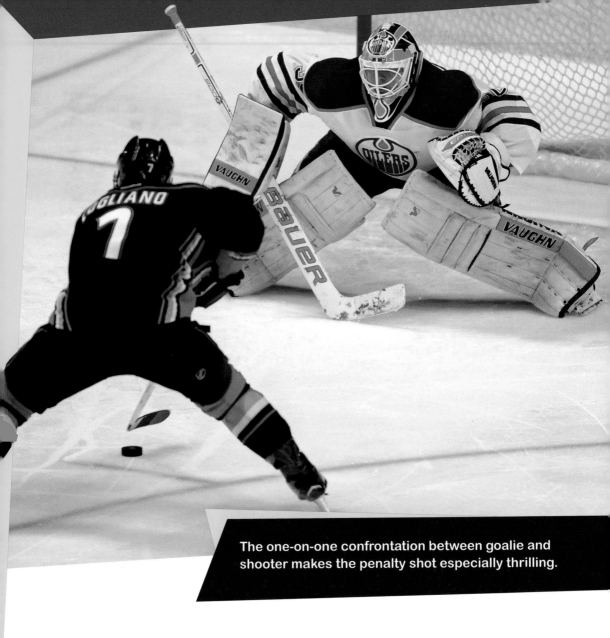

The one-on-one confrontation between goalie and shooter makes the penalty shot especially thrilling.

But fighting is dangerous. It can lead to concussions and other injuries. Fighting is not allowed in youth hockey. It's also not allowed in high school, college, or the Olympics. Many fans would like to see it banned from the NHL.

If a player is tripped to prevent a clear goal-scoring chance, the referee can award a penalty shot. That gives the player a one-on-one chance against the goalie. A penalty shot is one of the most exciting plays in hockey.

Brendan Shanahan is thought to be the all-time leader with 17 "Gordie Howe Hat Tricks." His 21-year career ended in 2009.

THE STANLEY CUP

It's one of the most famous trophies in sports. But unlike most trophies, there's only one Stanley Cup. The winners get possession of the actual Stanley Cup, not a replica. The captain of the winning team hoists it as his teammates go wild. Then it gets passed from player to player. Some kiss it. Some hug it. All cherish that moment. After all, most of them have been dreaming about it for their entire lives.

The Stanley Cup was originally just a bowl. A replica of that bowl now sits on top of the modern trophy. Lord Stanley of Preston, a British

Sidney Crosby, *center*, and his Pittsburgh Penguins gather around the Stanley Cup after winning the championship in 2016.

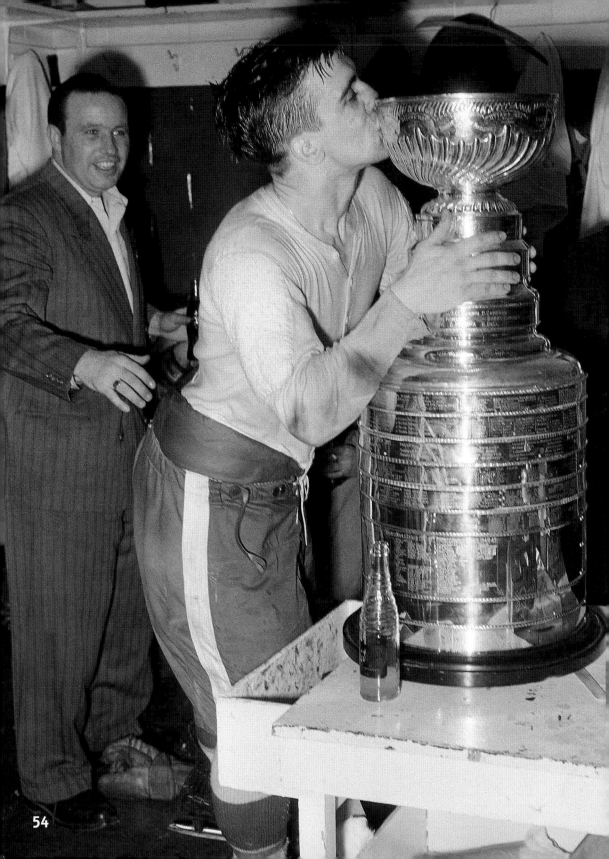

and Canadian politician, donated the cup in 1892 to be the championship trophy of Canada. The Montreal Amateur Athletic Association was the first winner in 1893. The cup was the championship trophy for several leagues. It got passed around to the winner of several postseason tournaments. The NHL took ownership of the trophy in 1926.

Jacques Plante won five NHL titles with Montreal. His name is spelled five different ways on the Cup.

Names of players on the Cup-winning team have been engraved on the cup every year since 1924. To make room, the bowl was affixed to a base with multiple rings. Because the trophy has been around for so long, even the rings ran out of space. Now, when a ring is filled with names, all rings move up a level. Then a blank one is added to the bottom. The top ring is "retired" and put

Ted Lindsay kisses the Stanley Cup after his Detroit Red Wings defeated the New York Rangers to win the title in 1950.

Two handlers from the Hockey Hall of Fame are assigned to travel with the Stanley Cup.

on display at the Hockey Hall of Fame in Toronto. The original bowl is also in the Hall of Fame.

The current cup is 35 1/4 inches (90 cm) tall and weighs 34 1/2 pounds (16 kg). The Montreal Canadiens have won it

23 times. Canadiens great Henri Richard has his name on the cup 11 times. That's the most of any player or coach.

The cup has had some mishaps over the years. Every player who wins it gets to spend a day with it during the summer. The cup has been lost, stolen, damaged, and even used to baptize a baby.

CUP ERRORS

The Stanley Cup has nearly 2,500 names engraved on it. There's bound to be a mistake or two. Almost all are spelling errors. The 1980–81 New York Islanders team name is spelled "ILANDERS." One of the strangest is the 1971–72 Boston Bruins. The city name used Qs instead of Os to make BQSTQN. After winning the Cup in 1984, Edmonton Oilers owner Peter Pocklington insisted his father's name be put on the trophy. But his father had no official role with the team. The NHL ordered his name to be crossed out.

12

WORKING THE PUCK

Hockey is a fast-paced game. Players need to make decisions quickly. They're almost always in motion. Players must quickly read the action on the ice and react.

On offense, a team should always be looking to attack the net. Forwards should be deep in the offensive zone. Defensemen guard the blue line. The key is to maintain possession. The longer a team has the puck, the more likely they'll score.

One way to keep possession is by cycling. Teams use the rounded shape of the corner

An offensive player gets pressure on both sides as he tries to get an open shot on goal.

A successful power play will create open shots and scoring opportunities.

boards to work the puck around the zone. A forward can pick it up behind the net when the puck rings the boards. The other offensive players work to get open in front of the net. A quick pass from behind the net can set up a great scoring opportunity for a teammate.

Defense is about matching up with the offensive players. Positions are reversed from offense. Defensemen play deep in the zone, covering the attacking forwards. Forwards have defensive responsibilities all over the zone. The goalie can help by handling the puck and passing to teammates if enough space is available.

If the defense can't take the puck away, it should force the offense to the edges of the zone. They should work to prevent forwards from getting free in front of the net. Defenders should also work to bump players off the puck and get their sticks in passing lanes.

POWER PLAY

Teams playing with an extra player generally have the puck for most of the power play. Quick, crisp passes will keep the defense chasing the puck. That will open space for forwards to get a shot. Shorthanded teams need to stay disciplined. Many teams set up in a "box" formation to cover the net. Players on the four corners of the box move as necessary to cover players or the puck.

GLOSSARY

amateur
Someone who is not paid to perform an activity.

faceoff
When a puck is dropped between one player from each team to restart play.

league
A collection of teams that compete against each other.

overtime
An extra period of play when the score is tied after regulation.

preseason
A period of time before a team's regular season starts in which games played do not count.

professional
Someone who is paid to perform an activity.

replica
A copy, not the original.

rink
An ice surface on which people skate.

FOR MORE INFORMATION

Books

Myers, Dan. *Hockey Trivia*. Minneapolis, MN: Abdo Publishing, 2016.

Myers, Jess. *Hockey Record Breakers*. Minneapolis, MN: Abdo Publishing, 2016.

Nagelhout, Ryan. *The Science of Hockey*. New York: PowerKids Press, 2016.

Websites

To learn more about hockey, visit **booklinks.abdopublishing.com**. These links are routinely monitored and updated to provide the most current information available.

INDEX

ABOUT THE AUTHOR

Todd Kortemeier studied journalism and English at the University of Minnesota and has authored dozens of books for young people, primarily on sports topics. He lives in Minneapolis, Minnesota, with his wife.